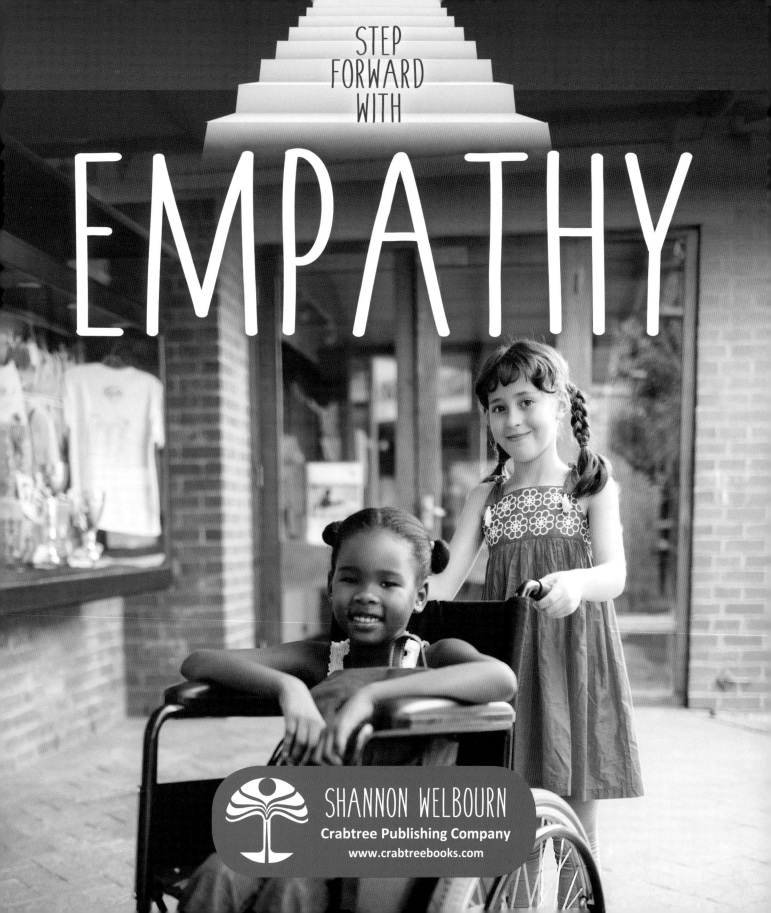

STEP
FORWARD
WITH

# EMPATHY

SHANNON WELBOURN

**Crabtree Publishing Company**
www.crabtreebooks.com

# STEP FORWARD!

**Author**
Shannon Welbourn

**Series research and development**
Reagan Miller

**Editorial director**
Kathy Middleton

**Editors**
Reagan Miller, Janine Deschenes

**Series Consultant**
Larry Miller: BA (Sociology), BPE, MSc.Ed
Retired teacher, guidance counselor, and certified coach

**Print and production coordinator**
Katherine Berti

**Design and photo research**
Katherine Berti

**Photographs**
Getty Images: JGI/Jamie Grill, front cover
Shutterstock: ©Lukas Maverick Greyson, p 14
Other images by Shutterstock

**Library and Archives Canada Cataloguing in Publication**

Welbourn, Shannon, author
    Step forward with empathy / Shannon Welbourn.

(Step forward!)
Includes index.
Issued in print and electronic formats.
ISBN 978-0-7787-2786-6 (hardback).--ISBN 978-0-7787-2827-6 (paperback).--
ISBN 978-1-4271-1831-8 (html)

    1. Empathy--Juvenile literature.  I. Title.

BF575.E55W45 2016          j152.4          C2016-903363-5
                                            C2016-903364-3

**Library of Congress Cataloging-in-Publication Data**

Names: Welbourn, Shannon, author.
Title: Step forward with empathy / Shannon Welbourn.
Description: New York : Crabtree Publishing Company, [2017] |
    Series: Step forward! | Includes index.
Identifiers: LCCN 2016034718 (print) | LCCN 2016043368 (ebook) |
    ISBN 9780778727866 (reinforced library binding : alk. paper) |
    ISBN 9780778728276 (pbk. : alk. paper) |
    ISBN 9781427118318 (Electronic HTML)
Subjects: LCSH: Empathy in children--Juvenile literature. |
    Empathy--Juvenile literature.
Classification: LCC BF723.E67 W45 2017 (print) | LCC BF723.E67 (ebook) |
    DDC 152.4/1--dc23
LC record available at https://lccn.loc.gov/2016034718

## Crabtree Publishing Company
www.crabtreebooks.com          1-800-387-7650

Printed in Canada/102016/IH20160811

**Published in Canada**
**Crabtree Publishing**
616 Welland Ave.
St. Catharines, Ontario
L2M 5V6

**Published in the United States**
**Crabtree Publishing**
PMB 59051
350 Fifth Avenue, 59th Floor
New York, New York 10118

**Published in the United Kingdom**
**Crabtree Publishing**
Maritime House
Basin Road North, Hove
BN41 1WR

**Published in Australia**
**Crabtree Publishing**
3 Charles Street
Coburg North
VIC 3058

# CONTENTS

# WHAT IS EMPATHY?

**Have you ever heard the saying "Try to put yourself in someone else's shoes"? This means that you should try to understand their point of view.**

Looking at things from another person's viewpoint helps you develop empathy. Empathy means thinking about what other people are thinking and feeling. When you **express** empathy, you have **compassion** for others. You show concern for their feelings.

*Empathy helps you understand others' feelings under different **circumstances**.*

We all have the ability to express empathy toward others. Empathy is a skill you can develop. You can show and develop empathy by taking time to listen to others express their feelings, and by being **respectful** of what they say. As you build your empathy, you become more aware of the people around you.

*Show your empathy by listening to what others have to say.*

# WHY IS EMPATHY IMPORTANT?

**Empathy is an important skill to develop. Learning to understand how someone else is feeling can help you build relationships.**

People who have empathy **value** the thoughts and feelings of others. To value something means to recognize that something is important. They show this by trying hard to understand why someone feels or acts in a certain way. People with empathy try to understand others' feelings before they react or respond to them. This helps them respond in a more thoughtful way.

*Showing empathy can help you build strong friendships throughout your life.*

When people use empathy to understand others' feelings, they build strong relationships. When you listen to someone's feelings, you show them that you can be trusted. Empathy can also help people avoid **conflict**, such as an argument. This is because they try to understand what makes others feel the way they do first, instead of reacting with anger. Approaching a problem with empathy can help you deal with it fairly.

# JAYDA SMITH-ATKINS

**Name:** Jayda Smith-Atkins

**From:** Halifax, Nova Scotia, Canada

**Accomplishment:** Helped give warm clothes to people without homes in her community.

**When Jayda Smith-Atkins felt the cold winter approaching, she knew that the people without homes in her** community **would need help.**

On her eighth birthday, Jayda decided to show empathy for people without homes in her community. Jayda felt the cold weather outside and imagined what it would be like to spend the winter without coats, mittens, scarves, and hats to keep warm. She put herself in the shoes of those without homes or warm clothing and knew that they needed help. With the help of her mother, Jayda collected old winter clothing from friends, family, and other members of her community.

She and seven of her friends set out on her birthday to leave the clothing around their community, so that people who need warmth could find the clothing easily. She and her friends put the needs of others before themselves. They showed amazing empathy by making warm clothing as accessible and useful as possible for others in their community. Amazingly, people around the world are also using this idea, and showing their empathy for others in their communities.

*Each piece of warm clothing had a tag attached so people knew they could use it to keep warm.*

# EMPATHY AT HOME

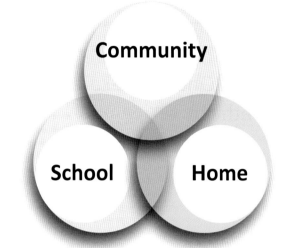

Community

School    Home

**Expressing empathy at home can help you build strong relationships with each member of your family.**

It's important for family members to feel that they are supported by each other. Try to show your support for your family by understanding their feelings. When all members of a family express empathy, they avoid conflict at home.

You may hear one of your family members talking about the bad day they had. You can express your empathy by offering to listen to them talk about their feelings. You can try to understand why they are upset. Maybe your little sister is upset because she lost her favorite toy. You might not understand why she is so upset, but you can show empathy by listening to her feelings before reacting to her **situation**. Once she explains how she feels, you can express your empathy by telling her about a time you felt the same way.

*Show your empathy at home by listening to your family members' feelings before you respond or react to problems.*

# EMPATHY AT SCHOOL

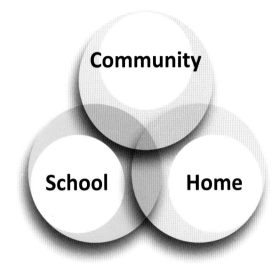

Community

School          Home

**Showing empathy at school helps others see that you can be a good friend.**

Show your classmates you care. Be understanding of them. Respect others' differences and think about how you are the same. Finding what you have in common can help you develop empathy.

## STEP FURTHER

What is one way that you can show a classmate that you respect their feelings?

We can show empathy at school by seeing things from our classmates' points of view.

Think of a time that someone put their hand up in class to answer a question. What happened if they gave an incorrect answer? How did others respond? Think of how you would respond. Maybe someone laughed or made a joke about the incorrect answer. Those responses would be hurtful, and do not show empathy. We can all relate to how it feels to raise your hand in class, or be called upon to answer. Sometimes it can be scary. Think about how you would feel if others laughed at your answer. Understanding how your classmate may feel in this type of situation helps you show empathy.

# EMPATHY IN YOUR COMMUNITY

Community

School     Home

**A community is a group of people who live, work, and play in a place. Your home, school, and neighborhood are parts of your community.**

Part of developing empathy is having **open-mindedness**. To be open-minded is to look at things from many different points of view and be accepting of many ways to think or do things. There are many different people in your community. You may not always know them.

When you are open-minded toward all of the people in your community, it means that you try to see their **perspective** before making your own **assumptions** about them. You can develop your open-mindedness by learning about many different types of people. Maybe you can join a new club or sit with a new group of students at lunch. Showing empathy in your community means that you take time to learn about people's situations, perspectives, and feelings.

*One way to show your empathy in your community is to help others. You could collect food or clothing to give to those who need it.*

DONATIONS

# BUDDY BENCHES

**Buddy Benches are tools that help children learn empathy. The bench encourages children to depend on each other, develop friendships, and listen to each others' feelings.**

When children are playing outside at recess, they could feel left out. Some children may feel lonely. Others may feel they do not belong. Buddy benches are places where children can sit when they need someone to talk to. Sitting on the bench is a way that children can show that they need help without saying it. When other children see someone sitting on the bench, they can can talk to the person on the bench or invite them to play.

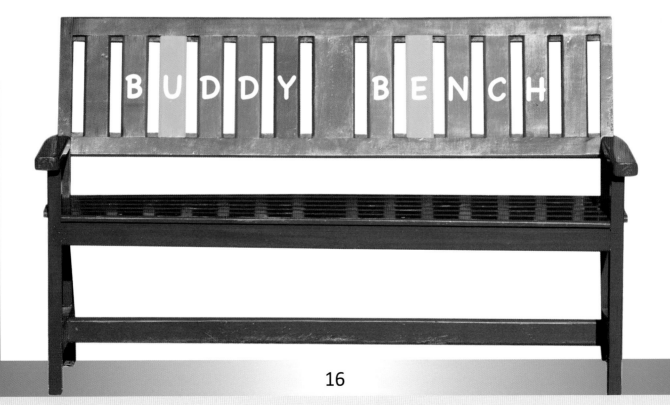

An important part of empathy is being able to understand other people's feelings, even if they do not say them out loud. Buddy Benches help kids develop this part of empathy because they recognize how a person might be feeling when they sit on the bench. Buddy Benches encourage children to express their empathy for each other by respectfully listening to others' feelings and relating to them.

*Buddy Benches can be found on playgrounds around the world. Children everywhere use them to feel included and develop empathy.*

# OVERCOMING CHALLENGES

**You will develop your empathy over time as you learn to accept others and appreciate differences.**

Showing empathy toward others is not something you do once and check off a list. It becomes a part of who you are as a person.

**The tips listed below can help you develop your empathy.**

- If you don't understand how someone is feeling, ask questions to help. Listen to their answers.

- Remember that listening is more than just hearing what others say—it is understanding what you hear.

- Relate to others by remembering a time that you felt the same way. Share your experiences with them.

- You can express empathy with your words and actions. You might say words of encouragement to someone or do something nice for them. Use both!

Think of a time someone showed you empathy. What words and actions did they express to you?

# ENCOURAGING EMPATHY IN OTHERS

**One of the best ways you can encourage empathy in others is by being a good example yourself.**

When you express empathy toward others, you are a **role model** for them to develop their empathy skills, too. Everyone can develop empathy.

### STEP FURTHER

What would you do if you saw someone who was not being respectful or thoughtful toward someone else?

Think back to the example of someone in class giving the wrong answer. If a classmate laughed at them, you can remind the classmate to think about how they would feel if they were in that person's shoes. It is important to not make assumptions about anyone before learning their point of view. Encourage others to look at situations from the other person's perspective. What might their thoughts and feelings be? Encourage kindness and understanding in every situation. Express your empathy!

# EMPATHY IN ACTION

**We show empathy by using words and actions that make people feel important, respected, and valued. We can grow and develop empathy with effort and practice.**

Read each situation described below and answer the following questions. Then, share your ideas with a friend.

- How do you think the people in each situation feel?
- What could you say and do to show empathy?

*Your brother studied very hard for a history test. When he gets the test back, his mark is much lower than he thought it would be.*

*Your soccer team wins the championship game in overtime. As you and your teammates cheer and celebrate, you see players from the other team standing quietly nearby.*

*A new student joins your class in the middle of the year. She is from a different country and knows only a few words in English. Other kids make fun of the way she speaks.*

# LEARNING MORE

## BOOKS

Ludwig, Trudy. *The Invisible Boy.* Knopf Books for Young Readers, 2013.

Martin, Martha. *Live It: Empathy.* Crabtree Publishing, 2010.

McGovern, Cammie. *Just My Luck.* Harper Collins, 2016.

Sornson, Bob. *Stand in My Shoes: Kids Learning About Empathy.* Love and Logic Press, 2013.

## WEBSITES

**http://bit.ly/1OhIKfh**
This site helps children identify and relate to different experiences and feelings. Video clips show children describing different emotions. Viewers try to identify the emotions being described.

**www.startempathy.org**
Explore student-powered projects that show the positive impact of empathy in schools.

**www.rootsofempathy.org**
This program helps children increase empathy at school.

# WORDS TO KNOW

**assumptions** [*uh*-SUHMP-sh*uh* ns] noun  Something that is supposed to be true without evidence; taken for granted

**circumstance** [SUR-kuhm-stans] noun  A condition or detail of a situation, time, or place

**community** [k*uh*-MYOO-ni-tee] noun  A group of people who live, work, and play in a place

**compassion** [kuhm-PASH-uhn] noun  Feeling concern for another

**conflict** [KON-flikt] noun  A clash or incompatible difference of ideas, interests, or goals

**express** [ik-SPRES] verb  To show or put into words and actions

**open-mindedness** [OH-p*uh* n-MAHYN-did-nes] noun  To be accepting of different ideas and perspectives

**perspective** [per-SPEK-tiv] noun  A person's view or way of thinking about something

**respectful** [ri-SPEKT-f*uh* l] adjective  Describing someone who is polite and gives appropriate attention to others

**role model** [rohl MOD-l] noun  A person who is respected by others

**situation** [sich-oo-EY-shuhn] noun  Circumstances or position at a given moment

**value** [VAL-yoo] verb  To place importance on something

# INDEX

# ABOUT THE AUTHOR

Shannon Welbourn is a freelance author of educational K-12 books. She holds an honors BA in Child & Youth Studies, and is a certified teacher. Shannon works full-time as a Library and Media Specialist. In this position, she works closely with teachers and teacher candidates, helping to inspire and develop a passion for learning. Shannon lives close to Niagara Falls and enjoys vacationing in the Muskokas with her family.